GUIDE TO

ECUADOR

MARION MORRISON

Consultants: Roslyn Cameron and Rosanna Rivadeneira Cordero

Highlights for Children

CONTENTS

On the cover: On Ecuador's Galápagos Islands, the land iguana spends much of its time sunning itself.

The publisher is grateful for the guidance of Roslyn Cameron, VIP Unit Manager, and Rosanna Rivadeneira Cordero, a journalist and public relations assistant, both from the Department of Institutional Development, Charles Darwin Research Station, Puerto Ayora, Santa Cruz, Galápagos Islands, Ecuador. Ms. Rivadeneira Cordero is a member of the Federación Nacional de Periodistas del Ecuador, a national federation of journalists in Ecuador.

Published by Highlights for Children
© 2004 Highlights for Children, Inc.
P.O. Box 18201
Columbus, Ohio 43218-0201
For information on *Top Secret Adventures*, visit
www.tsadventures.com or call 1-800-962-3661.

10 9 8 7 6 5 4 3 2 1
ISBN 0-87534-577-8

NORTH AMERICA

Tropic of Cancer

Equator

Ecuador

SOUTH AMERICA

Tropic of Capricorn

EUROPE

ASIA

AFRICA

AUSTRALIA

ANTARCTICA

△ **Ecuador's flag,** of yellow, blue, and red horizontal stripes, dates from the 1820s. With its neighboring countries Colombia and Venezuela, Ecuador was then part of the Republic of Gran Colombia. The flags of all three countries are still very similar. Ecuador's national emblem shows the Andean condor, Chimborazo Volcano, and the first steamboat built in Ecuador.

ECUADOR AT A GLANCE

Area 113,424 square miles (283,560 square kilometers)(includes Galápagos Islands)

Population 13,710,234

Capital Quito, population 1,399,814

Other big cities Guayaquil (2,013,500), Cuenca (276,964), Machala (198,123)

Highest mountain Mount Chimborazo Volcano, 20,696 feet (6,310 meters)

Longest river Napo, 530 miles (853 kilometers)

Largest lake San Pablo, 2 square miles (6 square kilometers)

Official language Spanish

▽ **Ecuador stamps** These stamps depict the beautiful landscape and flowers of the mainland and the Galápagos Islands, an Ecuadorian tennis star, and the country's naval history.

◁ **Ecuador money** The currency of Ecuador used to be *sucres.* The 5,000-*sucres* bank note showed Galápagos wildlife. Now the currency is U.S. dollars and cents. U.S.-dollar bank notes and both U.S. and special Ecuador cent coins are used and accepted in shops and banks.

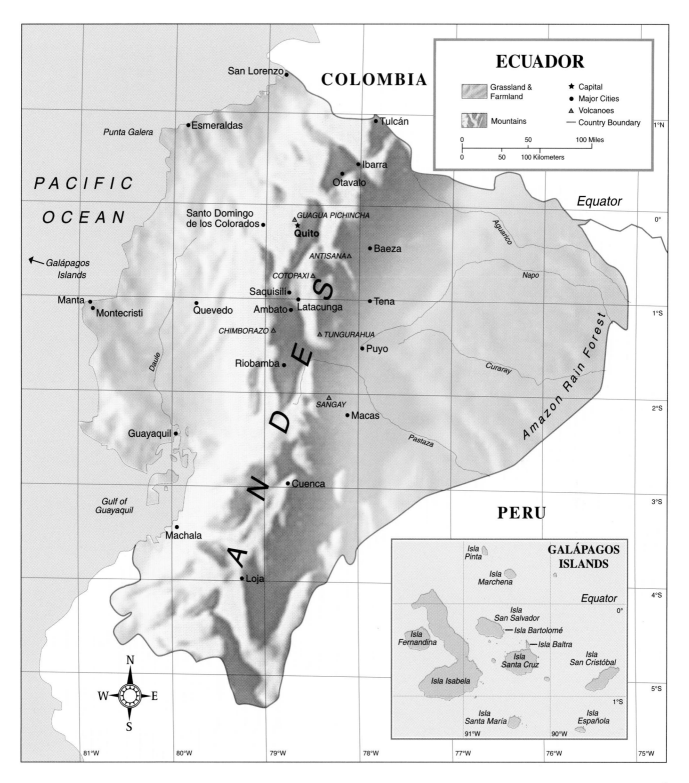

PACIFIC

OCEAN

COLOMBIA

PERU

ECUADOR

Grassland & Farmland

Mountains

★ Capital
● Major Cities
▲ Volcanoes
— Country Boundary

0   50   100 Miles
0   50   100 Kilometers

1°N

Equator

0°

1°S

2°S

3°S

San Lorenzo

Punta Galera

Esmeraldas

Tulcán

Ibarra

Otavalo

Santo Domingo de los Colorados

GUAGUA PICHINCHA

Quito

ANTISANA

Baeza

Aguarico

Napo

COTOPAXI

Saquisilí

Latacunga

Tena

Galápagos Islands

Manta

Montecristi

Quevedo

Ambato

CHIMBORAZO

TUNGURAHUA

Puyo

Curaray

Amazon Rain Forest

A N D E S

Daule

Riobamba

SANGAY

Macas

Pastaza

Guayaquil

Cuenca

Gulf of Guayaquil

Machala

Loja

N
W   E
S

GALÁPAGOS ISLANDS

Isla Pinta

Isla Marchena

Equator

0°

Isla San Salvador
— Isla Bartolomé

Isla Fernandina

— Isla Baltra

Isla Santa Cruz

Isla San Cristóbal

Isla Isabela

1°S

Isla Santa María

Isla Española

91°W

90°W

81°W   80°W   79°W   78°W   77°W   76°W   75°W

4°S

5°S

WELCOME TO ECUADOR

The Republic of Ecuador is one of South America's smallest countries. To the north, east, and south, Ecuador is dwarfed by the much larger republics of Colombia and Peru. To the west lies the Pacific Ocean. The Andes Mountains run north to south through its center. Some 600 miles (960 kilometers) from the coast are Ecuador's Galápagos Islands.

Ecuador takes its name from the equator. This is the imaginary line that circles the earth, dividing the world into the Northern and Southern Hemispheres. Ecuador has some of the highest volcanoes in the world. Cotopaxi, 19,342 feet (5,897 meters), and Chimborazo, 20,696 feet (6,310 meters), are perhaps the best known. In the east of the country is mainly rain forest and cloud forest, crossed by countless rivers that run into the Amazon River. Few people live here, only small groups of Native South Americans and settlers who have arrived with the oil, timber, and farming industries.

The capital, Quito, and most major cities are in the highlands. This is also where the majority of people live. Most Ecuadorians are descendants of mixed marriages between Spanish explorers and Native South Americans. Ecuador's largest city, Guayaquil, is on the coast, where it has become the country's major port around the Guayas River. Here, many people have African roots and traditions because they are descended from African slaves who arrived in the 1800s.

Evidence of some of South America's oldest civilizations—thousands of years old—has been found on Ecuador's coast. In the late 1400s, the Inca people from Peru conquered most of the country. Then the Spaniards arrived, and Ecuador was a Spanish colony for almost 300 years. In 1830, it became an independent republic. Since then, Ecuador has survived some troubled political and economic times, but today it is an increasingly popular destination for tourists.

▷ **Guayaquil, Ecuador's largest city** Founded in the 1530s, it is the country's chief seaport. Guayaquil handles about 90 percent of all Ecuador's imports and 50 percent of its exports.

▽ **The San Rafael Falls** This is Ecuador's highest waterfall. It is surrounded by rain forest on the Quijos River in the eastern range of the Andes Mountains.

▽ **The Saquisilí weekly market** People come from miles around and bring produce of every kind for sale, including piglets like these.

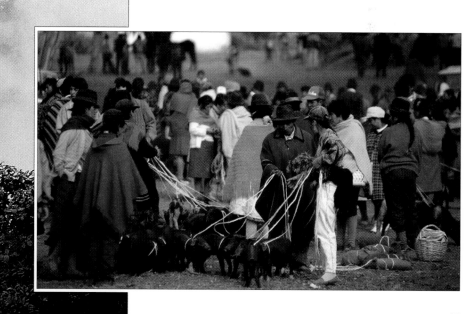

7

CITY OF ETERNAL SPRING

Ecuador's capital, Quito, is 9,350 feet (2,850 meters) above sea level and has pleasant springlike weather for most of the year. It lies in a valley at the foot of the active Guagua Pichincha Volcano, which has erupted at least twenty-five times. Quito takes its name from the Quitus people, who lived there in pre-Columbian times. It was founded in 1534 by the Spaniard Sebastián de Benalcázar at the site of an old Incan city.

Quito is divided into the Old and New City. At the heart of the Old City and historic center is the main square, the Plaza de la Independencia. The Cathedral and Presidential Palace occupy two sides of the square. Every day young shoeshine boys and street traders selling all kinds of trinkets fill the plaza.

In nearby streets stand two of Quito's most magnificent colonial churches, the Jesuit Church of La Compañia, with its fine carved facade, and the Church of San Francisco, Quito's largest church. La Compañia's main treasure, a painting of the Virgin framed in emeralds and gold, is so precious, it is kept in a bank. Walking along the cobbled streets, among colonial houses, is fascinating, but you can get breathless because the town is so high above sea level.

Plenty of buses and taxis run between the Old and New City, which, as its name suggests, is filled with modern high-rises and glass-and-concrete office buildings. The streets and avenues are broad and lined with trees. Here, you will find outdoor cafés, fashionable shops, and some grand houses.

There are over 86 churches in Quito and many museums. Located in Parque El Ejido, the Casa de la Cultura Ecuatoriana has exhibits of Ecuador's modern art, traditional dress, and musical instruments. Most impressive are the archeological exhibits of ceramic and gold objects created by Ecuador's early cultures.

△ **The Jesuit Church of La Compañia in Quito** La Compañia is famous for its very fine, ornately carved facade. It also has a magnificent gilded interior with a high altar plated in gold.

▷ **Guards in 1800s military uniform** These guards are on duty outside the Presidential Palace in Quito.

▽ **Quito, Ecuador's capital** This view to the northwest overlooks the new part of the city, where there are many office buildings as well as the financial center. In the distance is Guagua Pichincha Volcano.

THE MIDDLE OF THE WORLD

On the weekends, many Ecuadorians head north on the paved Pan American Highway from Quito to the colorful Otavalo market. On the way, the Avenue Manuel Cordova Galarza leads to the Mitad del Mundo monument. This marks the exact spot, determined by French scientist Charles-Marie de la Condamine in 1736, of the equator line, or the middle of the world.

The Otavaleño Native South Americans are a very successful people. They are traditionally weavers, and some 50,000 Otavaleños work in the trade. They produce all kinds of knitted and woven goods and travel to many parts of the world to sell them. Their craft market is held in the Plaza de los Ponchos in Otavalo. One area of the market is devoted to fruit and vegetables, while the Saturday morning cattle market takes place a short distance outside of town. Many Otavaleños now have their own homes and businesses and send their children to school and college.

Despite their success, the Otavaleños remain in many ways unchanged. Their children learn the Quichua native language before they learn Spanish. They still wear traditional dress. The men have white calf-length trousers and deep blue ponchos. Women's dress includes delicately embroidered blouses, colorful shawls, ankle-length deep blue skirts, woven belts, and masses of gold-bead necklaces. Both men and women have thick black hair, which they wear in a single braid.

The Chota Valley north of Otavalo is known for its sugar. It is also the home of descendants of the only Ecuadorian highland group of black African slaves. Other towns such as Ibarra and Cotacachi produce many crafts, for example, wood carvings, bread figures, and leather goods. The region is mountainous and includes Ecuador's third-highest volcano, Cayambe, at 18,991 feet (5,790 meters). It is the highest point that lies directly on the equator.

▽ **Cayambe Volcano** The volcano overlooks cultivated Andean slopes, where many productive dairy farms turn out some tasty cheeses.

▷ **The Mitad del Mundo monument** A yellow line marks the exact location of the equator. Place one foot on each side of the line, and you are standing in the Northern and Southern Hemispheres at the same time.

▽ **Young Otavalo girl in traditional dress** Wearing her embroidered blouse, long skirt, and many strings of beads, a young Otavaleño works in the market.

11

AFRO-ECUADOR

A highway connects Ibarra in the center of the north to San Lorenzo on the north coast. (A railroad train had made a similar trip but is no longer in service because of landslides.) The highway passes through cloud forests and rain forests that in places have been widely destroyed by settlers and ranching. Elsewhere, the tropical forests are home to species of wildlife similar to those found in the Amazon forests to the east. These include mammals and rodents such as the tapir and the capybara, monkeys, and colorful birds that include toucans, macaws, and parrots.

African slaves were brought to Ecuador in the 1800s and 1900s to work on the cacao and banana plantations. They traveled by way of the Panama Canal and south through the Pacific Ocean to the coasts of Colombia and Ecuador. Today, San Lorenzo is a center of black culture, particularly music played on a marimba, an instrument similar to a xylophone.

The people of the region are known as *mulattos*—people of mixed African and European descent—and *montuvios*, who are of mixed white, Native South American, and black descent. Ecuadorian Native South American Indians include the Cuaiquers, who live on a reserve near the Colombian border, and an isolated group called the Cayapas in the remote northwest corner of Ecuador.

◁ **A tapir in the tropical forest** Tapirs look like a mix of a pig and an elephant, but their closest relatives are horses and rhinoceroses. They are active mainly at night, feeding on grasses, leaves, buds, and fruits.

▷ **A gold mask from the La Tolita civilization** This mask is now the emblem of Ecuador's national bank and shows a sun god with rays radiating from the head.

A new, mostly paved highway connects San Lorenzo to the town of Esmeraldas. A few miles south of Esmeraldas, Atacames is one of the most popular beaches on this part of the coast. An island not far from Esmeraldas was the center of the La Tolita culture that lasted from about 500 B.C. to A.D. 500. On the island, archaeologists have found many copper, platinum, and gold objects created by the La Tolita people.

◁ **An Afro-Ecuadorian woman selling fruit** In many towns and villages in the north, you will see Ecuadorians of a wide variety of cultures and origins.

13

AVENUE OF THE VOLCANOES

The route back to the highlands from the coast passes through the town of Santo Domingo de los Colorados. This was once the home of the Colorado (colored) Native South Americans. The name describes their custom of dying their hair and bodies with the red color of the achiote plant.

The Pan American Highway is the best way to see the "Avenue of the Volcanoes." The German scientist Alexander von Humboldt was the first to give Ecuador's central valley its popular name after he arrived in 1802. Nineteen volcanoes line the west of the valley, and 20 volcanoes line the eastern side. The most impressive volcano is Cotopaxi, approximately 18 miles (29 kilometers) from Latacunga.

The most popular excursion from Latacunga is to the Cotopaxi National Park. Many people go there to walk or cycle, but the more adventurous climb the volcano.

Another tour from Latacunga is around the Quilotoa circuit, which includes several villages and takes two or three

◁ **A Colorado man** The man's red-colored hair is dyed from the achiote plant. The Colorados now live in communities on a reservation near Santo Domingo de los Colorados, and there are fewer than 2,000 of them left.

▷ **Cotopaxi Volcano** The volcano is 19,342 feet (5,897 meters) high. It is one of the world's highest active volcanoes.

days by bus. A particular highlight is the Thursday market at Saquisilí, where stalls are stocked with handicrafts created by artists, as well as fruit, vegetables, and meat.

An old highway from Latacunga passes through the pretty towns of Pilaló and El Tingo. Unusual, tall plants of the *páramo* (high plains) are often shrouded by mist, and cloud forests cover the mountain slopes. Lower down, the road crosses the mountain foothills, where there are forests of balsa wood trees. Balsa wood, which is very light when dry, is used all over the world for making architectural models, model aircraft, and small boxes.

Quevedo is the only sizeable town along the route and is surrounded by banana plantations. The town is known as the Chinatown of Ecuador because many Chinese immigrants settled there. Signs with Chinese characters and names are everywhere, advertising everything from dentists to cement distributors and clothing shops.

▽ **A sign at an entrance to Cotopaxi National Park** In the park the volcanoes Cotopaxi and Rumiñahui are surrounded by beautiful scenery.

LAND OF THE PANAMA HAT

Along the central coast, Manta is Ecuador's second-largest seaport and a busy commercial center. In Manta, it is a fascinating experience to watch the fishing boats return early in the morning. Fish of many shapes and sizes are brought ashore. The beach is crowded with sellers and buyers shouting prices at each other.

For many years people believed, understandably, that Panama hats came from Panama, in Central America. This is not so. The real home of the woven-straw Panama hat is a small Ecuadorian town close to Manta, called Montecristi.

△ **Making a Panama hat** Miners traveling through Panama on their way to California during the gold rush in the mid–1800s gave this kind of hat its name. They assumed that the hats were made there. But they were, and still are, made in Ecuador.

◁ **The early morning fish market in Manta** The fish are brought in soon after dawn and include sardines, tuna, whitefish, anchovies, and shrimp.

◁ **Guayaquil's largest plaza** Watermelon sellers pass through the Parque del Centenario. The park contains the monument Liberty, a city landmark.

In Montecristi, people make the hats by hand from the very fine fronds of a native plant, called *La Carluduvica Palmata,* that grows best near Guayaquil. The fronds are boiled and then dried in the sun. Hats of the best quality, using the finest straw, take up to three months to make. Sadly, fewer people are learning the skill of hat making because they do not make enough money from selling them.

Traveling along the coast road from Manta to Guayaquil, you pass through several sites of Ecuador's ancient civilizations. Among them is Valdivia, which, at some 5,000 years old, is said to be the oldest site in South America.

Also on this coast is the Machalilla National Park, which includes the Isla de la Plata and some fine beaches. Many visitors come to the Isla between June and September to watch the acrobatics of humpback whales. The whales travel some 5,000 miles (over 8,000 kilometers) from the icy cold waters of the Antarctic in search of mating partners.

Guayaquil is Ecuador's largest city, with a population of more than 2 million, and is its major seaport. It is a bustling city, and it can be unbearably hot. Few tourists spend much time here. The lucky ones head off for the Galápagos Islands.

GALÁPAGOS ISLANDS

Most people fly to the Galápagos, although you can take a cargo ship from Guayaquil. The journey by sea lasts an average of four days. Once at the islands, visitors can choose live-aboard tours on local vessels. Or those staying in hotels can explore the islands with day-tour operators. Visitors are restricted by the national park authorities to 52 landing sites, each with a well-defined trail. The islands are a UNESCO World Heritage site, and every effort is made to protect them.

The Galápagos consist of 13 large and 6 small volcanic islands and more than 40 islets. None has ever been attached to the mainland. This is important because it has allowed the wildlife on the islands to develop in complete isolation, and many of the animals are found only on Galápagos. The British scientist and naturalist Charles Darwin visited the islands in 1835. Darwin's observations of the animals formed an important part of his theory of evolution during his later years. He noted how the animals had adapted to their environment and, in some cases, how the same animal developed in different forms on different islands.

The island's many species of finch helped Darwin develop his theory. Each species survived by feeding on a particular type of food, for example, seeds, berries, or insects, in order to avoid competing.

Small groups of people have lived on the islands since the early 1800s. Despite increasing numbers of immigrants from mainland Ecuador, the animals are still unafraid. Although you cannot touch them, you can approach them. There are giant tortoises weighing more than 440 pounds (200 kilograms) and marine and land iguanas. The birdlife includes species such as the blue-footed booby, which offers a magnificent courtship display, as well as cormorants, albatrosses, finches, and gulls.

▷ **Volcanic islands** Bartolomé Island is part of the Galápagos group of islands, formed by underwater volcanoes. The island is uninhabited but popular with tourists. Its well-known Pinnacle Rock provides fine panoramic views. Off the island's beach you can swim and snorkel with penguins.

▷ **The Galápagos giant tortoise** The shape of the tortoise's shell reminded the early Spaniards of a type of horse-riding saddle they called *galápago*. That is how the tortoises were named. In turn, the islands were named for the many thousands of turtles that once roamed there.

▽ **Blue-footed boobies in the Galápagos** Boobies are excellent fishers. They dive into the water at great speed, folding their wings before entry.

STEEP HIGHLANDS AND FERTILE LOWLANDS

A spectacular railroad, opened in 1908, runs from Durán, near Guayaquil, to the highlands. Engineers had to build it in such a way that trains could pull carriages up and down the steep slopes of the Andes Mountains. In one section it climbs about 10,000 feet (over 3,000 meters) in 50 miles (80 kilometers).

Parts of the railroad line were damaged when Ecuador's coast suffered from the flooding caused by the El Niño ocean current in the late 1990s. The train journey, nicknamed the Good and Quick, is still popular but not so reliable. The alternative is a bus to Ambato.

The coastal lowlands are some of the most fertile parts of Ecuador, particularly around the Guayas Valley. Endless fields of sugarcane stretch to the horizon, inhabited only by workers' palm-stilted houses or sugar mills. The hot climate and frequent rains are also good for rice production. For years the area has also been important for cacao, from which chocolate is made. Cacao was Ecuador's most important export in the early 1900s, and it was because of this industry that the railway was built.

Banana plantations, too, are everywhere. Ecuador is one of the world's leading producers of bananas. Each

◁ **Rice fields** Rice is grown in parts of the coastal lowlands, where there is enough rainfall. Some rice is exported, but most is for local distribution and consumption.

▷ **Chimborazo Volcano** The volcano is Ecuador's highest mountain. It was first climbed by the British mountaineer Edward Whymper in 1880.

▷ **Hands of bananas** Once picked, the bananas are inspected for quality before they are shipped to markets.

plantation has a collecting point where workers wash, dry, and pack the bananas, readying them for the trucks that take them to Guayaquil. Many other fruits also grow in the lowlands. Along the roadside are dozens of stalls piled high with oranges, pineapples, melons, plantains, and papayas.

Leaving behind the lowlands, the winding road leads up the valley of the Ambato River and over a high area of desert called the Gran Arenal. The road passes by the volcanoes Chimborazo and Carihuairazo. Large, dark, brooding Chimborazo is often covered in clouds, and mountaineers say it is difficult to climb.

A great earthquake in 1949 destroyed much of Ambato and some surrounding villages. The city has been largely rebuilt, and streets are lined with trees. Because of its large flower and agriculture business, Ambato is known as the City of Flowers and Fruits.

The Pan American Highway runs south, connecting Ambato with Riobamba. Just a short distance from Ambato, the highway passes through the village of Salasaca, named after the Native South Americans who live there. They dress in white trousers, broad white hats, and distinctive black ponchos. The Salasacas are farmers, but they are famed for their fabrics woven with designs of birds and animals.

There is an alternative route east to the lowland town of Baños, a favorite vacation spot for people from the highlands and for foreign tourists. Baños is a small town of about 16,000 people. Some 5,910 feet (1,800 meters) above sea level, it has a relaxing, warm climate and is filled with outdoor cafés, restaurants, and hotels. It also has five sets of thermal baths, and children love the hot springs. People come here to walk or for river rafting. Many rivers and waterfalls are nearby. One of the most spectacular is the Devil's Cauldron. Baños is also a base for climbing Tungurahua Volcano, at 16,475 feet (5,023 meters), and for exploring the jungles of the east.

The highway route to Riobamba is marked by a large sculpture of a macaw and a toucan. Riobamba is the capital of Chimborazo Province and has many interesting museums and churches. Heading south from Riobamba, the scenery changes. There are green mountain slopes and deep valleys covered with pastures, some forests, and cultivated fields.

▽ **Town center of Baños** The local thermal baths and nearby rain forest attract visitors.

▷ **Ecuadorian woman from the Salasaca community spinning wool** Wooden looms are used for weaving the wool into cloth, much of which is sold to tourists.

▽ **Traveling by truck** Few local people have cars, and without a reliable bus service, many Salasaca Indians get around by truck.

THE SOUTH

On the road between Riobamba and Cuenca, the southern capital, is the small town of Cañar. It is named after the once-powerful Cañaris people, who fought fiercely against the Spaniards. Although primarily farmers, Cañaris still make beautiful woven belts and ponchos. The women's clothes are colorfully embroidered, and it is possible to know which village the women come from by the distinctive style of their hats.

Other Native South Americans in the far south of Ecuador include the Saraguros. They have a reputation as good cattle breeders and traders, and they migrate every year with their herds to the lowlands, looking for pastureland.

Ingapirca, Ecuador's most important Inca ruin, is close to Cañar. The site has served various purposes. It has housed a temple. It has been a stopping place for travelers between the Inca capital, Cusco, in Peru, and Quito. And it has been used by the Spaniards as a fortress.

Cuenca is Ecuador's third-largest city and the intellectual and economic center of the south. It has many fine buildings, including several churches and the new cathedral begun in 1880. Walking around the city is a delight. Whitewashed buildings line the cobblestone streets, and plazas are filled with flowers. The most beautiful festival in Cuenca takes place on the Saturday before Christmas, when children decorate donkeys and vehicles with all kinds of produce and gifts. Then they parade through the town, many of them dressed to look like people described in the Bible.

Two of Ecuador's national parks are in the south—Cajas, near Cuenca, and Podocarpus. Both have incredible birdlife, and Podocarpus is one of the few habitats of the Andean spectacled bear. Also in the far south are the well-known towns of Loja and Vilcabamba. Loja is where cinchona, the tree containing quinine, a cure for the tropical disease malaria, was first discovered. Vilcabamba is famed for the very long lives enjoyed by the people who live there.

▽ **The Inca ruins at Ingapirca** Today, the ruins consist of a roofless, round stone-wall building. Nearby are particular rock formations known as the Inca's Playground, Inca's Face, and Inca's Chair.

△ **Saraguros dressed mainly in black** It is said that these Native South Americans wear somber colors because they are in permanent mourning for the Inca Emperor Atahualpa, killed by the Spanish in the 1500s.

△ **Cuenca Cathedral** The brightly colored domes of the new cathedral, built in the 1880s, dominate the skyline of the city.

THE ORIENTE

The easy way to get back to Quito from Cuenca is by air. But a much longer and more fascinating route is through the Oriente. It is possible to make the whole journey by road, but it is quicker and less hazardous to cover some sections by air.

The Oriente is vast. It occupies almost half of Ecuador. Much of it is covered by Amazon rain forest, lakes, and rivers. Roads are difficult to build, and in many places only river transport is possible. Few people live in the region, although it has been home to forest-dwelling Native South Americans for centuries, long before the Spaniards arrived. Six groups of these people have survived. The largest is the Quichua, with about 60,000 people. The Achuar have 30,000, and the other groups each have fewer than 10,000 people.

The Native South Americans' traditional way of life has had to change with the arrival of oil workers, missionaries, settlers, and tourists. Once they lived almost entirely from the rain forest. Now they have to adapt to Western ideas. The Achuar, for example, are encouraging ecotourism so that visitors can enjoy the forest, its plants, and its animals without hurting the

◁ **Student tourists on Cuyabeno Lake in the northern Oriente** The lake is in the Cuyabeno Wildlife Reserve. There, you can see a large variety of wildlife, including river dolphins, tapirs, capybaras, and caimans (the South American alligator).

▷ **An ocelot in the rain forest** This species of cat is endangered as a result of illegal hunting for its skin, used to make coats.

environment. The greatest damage and changes have been brought by cattle ranching and the oil and timber industries. Large areas of the forest have been destroyed, rivers have been polluted, and the local people have lost land to the developers.

One of the major oil centers is Lago Agrio in the northern Oriente. From here a pipeline has been built over the Andes to Esmeraldas on the coast. Quito is only a few hours away from here. On the way there, be sure to pass by the San Rafael Falls. Despite the changes in the area, the waterfall remains a fantastic sight in the heart of the forest.

◁ **Young Native South American girl** This girl lives in the Amazon rain forest near the Napo River. Many Native Americans now wear Western dress and use traditional dress only on special occasions.

27

ECUADOR FACTS AND FIGURES

People

Over half of Ecuadorians are *mestizos*, mixed-race descendents of Spanish settlers and Native South Americans. About a quarter are Native South Americans and include the Otavaleños, Salasaca, Cañaris, and Saraguros. Native South Americans in the Amazonian forests include the Quichua and the Achuar. Afro-Ecuadorians are people of mixed black, Native South American, and white descent. They live mostly on the coast. Many people in Ecuador live and work on farms and are known as *campesinos,* or "country people."

Trade and Industry

Ecuador's economy was based on agriculture until the mid-1900s, when large oil deposits were discovered in the northern Oriente. Oil exports now account for nearly half the country's income. However, despite the large reserves of oil, over half of Ecuador's energy is provided by hydroelectric power. Minerals include gold, silver, lead, zinc, and copper.

△ **Children from the Andean highlands**
These youngsters are *campesinos*.

Guayaquil and Quito are the main centers of manufacturing. Factories make items associated with agriculture, such as processed foods and drinks, and products derived from the petroleum industry. Tanneries produce leather goods. Panama hats are perhaps Ecuador's most famous export.

Farming

Ecuador is one of the world's top producers of bananas. Other crops grown on the coast include cacao, coffee, rice, sugar, and African oil palms, which produce vegetable oils. Ranches raise beef cattle. In the highlands, many of the farms are small. Families grow their own potatoes, barley, wheat, and beans and keep sheep, pigs, and dairy cattle. New cash crops such as strawberries, asparagus, and roses have helped to diversify the agricultural economy. In the highlands, plastic greenhouses cover many acres where the fruit, vegetables, and flowers are grown. Cut flowers are now an important export.

Fishing

Sardines, anchovies, and tuna are some of the fish caught on the Ecuador coast. Tuna is exported, but Ecuador's claims to offshore rights have led to disputes with the United States. Shrimp farming is a fairly new and successful industry.

Food

Soups include many different ingredients. The four soups listed below are very popular: *locro,* with cheese, avocado, and potato; *sancocho,* with meat, manioc, green plantains, and corn; *chupe de pescado*, with fish, potatoes, and carrots; and *fanesca,* a traditional soup for Easter made with fish, grain, and vegetables. In the highlands, rice, corn, and potatoes are staple foods eaten with beef, chicken, and pork. *Picante*, a hot pepper sauce, is used to spice up every meal. *Ceviche*, the favorite fish dish from the coast, is raw or cooked fish marinated in lime and served with onions and chili peppers. *Llapingachos,* potato patties with cheese inside, are served with a main dish. Snacks include *empanadas*, hot pastries filled with meat or cheese. The most exotic Ecuadorian dish, considered a delicacy, is roasted guinea pig.

Schools
Ecuadorian children should attend school from the age of six, but many do not. Parents need them to work and help the family, and schools in rural areas are often very distant. Many schools do not have adequate teaching materials and have too few teachers. Even in the cities, the day is split so that some pupils attend in the

△ **Weaving blankets** On looms in community workshops, the Salasaca people make blankets and clothes for sale in markets.

morning and others in the afternoon. The literacy rate, however, is high, with about 90 percent of the population able to read and write. Two native groups, the Otavaleños and the Saraguros, have succeeded in sending many of their children to colleges and universities.

The Media
Daily newspapers are published in several cities. In Quito, *El Comercio* and *Ultimas Noticias* have the biggest circulation, and in

Guayaquil, *El Universo* is the most widely read. There are also many magazines covering topics from hobbies to sports. Ecuador has five national television stations and many local stations. News and sports are also received by cable and satellite TV. There are over 300 radio stations.

Visual Arts
The ancient civilizations of coastal Ecuador fashioned fine jewelry and masks in gold, copper, and platinum and figurines in ceramic. Today, the Otavaleños and Salasacas are known for their weavings. Ibarra is famous for its wood-carvers, and Cotacachi is noted for its leatherwork. Brightly painted bread figures come from the town of Calderón. The most beautiful ceramics are made by the Canelos, Quichua Native South Americans. Ecuador's best-known artist, Oswaldo Guayasamín, often depicted the plight and suffering of Ecuadorians who live in poverty. It is a theme shared by other contemporary painters, including Eduardo Kingman.

ECUADOR FACTS AND FIGURES

Music and Dance

Ecuadorian music has Native South American and Spanish roots. Native South American instruments include the flute-like *quena*, panpipes, and drums. The Spanish introduced guitars, violins, and harps. The main highland dance is the *sanjuanito*. Men play while women sing and dance. Music on the coast has African roots. The main instrument is the marimba, which is like a xylophone, and it is accompanied by drums, rattles, and maracas. *Cumbia* music from Colombia as well as salsa are very popular.

Festivals

January 1 **New Year's Day**
January 6 **Epiphany**
February-March **Carnival**
May 1 **Labor Day**
May 24 **Battle of Pichincha**
July 24 **Birthday of Simón Bolívar**
August 10 **Independence Day**
October 12 **Columbus Day**
November 1–2 **All Souls' Day**
December 6 **Foundation of Quito**
December 29–31 **Year's End**

△ **Quichua musicians in *fiesta*, or festival, costumes** Groups of musicians playing guitars, rattles, and drums often tour villages and towns.

Religious holidays include **Easter** and **Christmas.**

Sports

Ecuador's favorite sport is *futbol*, or soccer. People will play or watch a game whenever and wherever they can. There are opportunities to play most sports. The natural environment is particularly good for climbers, trekkers, and hikers or for river rafting, kayaking, and canoeing. Off the coast, there is good surfing and other watersports. Andrés Gomez, a professional tennis player, is one of Ecuador's most successful athletes.

Plants

In the Amazon cloud forests and rain forests are tens of thousands of species of plants, and scientists are still finding new species. Ecuador's national tree is the cinchona. Quinine from its bark is used to fight malaria. In the coastal lowlands there are small forests of balsa wood. Ecuador's only conifer trees, Podocarpus, relics of a past age, are protected in a national park. The snowy slopes of volcanoes have their own specialized plants.

Animals

The giant tortoises, iguanas, sea lions, crabs, insects, and birds of the Galápagos Islands are unique and extraordinary. They are very different from the animals found in the Amazon forest, such as the tapir, capybara, monkey, caiman (alligator), toucan, and macaw. In the highlands, llamas and alpacas are reared for their wool and meat. The mountains are also home to spectacled bears, foxes, deer, and birds, including Ecuador's national bird, the Andean condor.

HISTORY

Some of the oldest known civilizations in South America lived on the Ecuador coast. The oldest, Valdivia, is about 5,000 years old. The Incas invaded from Peru in 1460 but were defeated by the Spanish, who conquered much of Ecuador in the 1530s.

Ecuador was a Spanish colony for about 300 years. The Spanish settlers took most of the land and enslaved the Native South Americans. They were forced to work on the farms and in gold mines. African slaves first arrived in the 1700s.

Ecuador became independent of Spain in 1822 and a republic in 1830. For much of the 1800s the Liberal and Conservative political parties battled for power. There was great rivalry between Guayaquil, supporting the Liberals, and Quito, the Conservatives. Peace was achieved for a while under General Eloy Alfaro, president from 1897 to 1901 and from 1906 to 1911. But troubles continued, and between 1923 and 1948 Ecuador had more than 20 presidents.

During the past century, there were periods of military rule, but one man, Dr. José María Velasco Ibarra, dominated the political scene. He was elected president five times, but only once did he complete his term.

Since 1979, governments have been democratically elected. The oil boom of the 1970s helped the country, but in the latter part of the twentieth century the effects began to fade. Social problems and guerrilla activity increased. The government also faced the problems of poverty and the economy. In recent years inflation has been reduced, and attempts have been made to improve the education of the poor.

LANGUAGE

Spanish, the official language of Ecuador, is spoken and understood widely in the country. But for more than 2 million people, Quichua is still their native language. These people come from the highlands, but Quichua, of which there are two or three dialects, is also used by people living in the Oriente. Other communities in the Oriente, such as the Achuar and the Siona, have their own languages. A small number of immigrants speak Chinese.

Useful words and phrases

English	Spanish
one	uno
two	dos
three	tres
four	cuatro
five	cinco
six	seis
seven	siete
eight	ocho
nine	nueve
ten	diez
Sunday	domingo
Monday	lunes
Tuesday	martes

Useful words and phrases

English	Spanish
Wednesday	miércoles
Thursday	jueves
Friday	viernes
Saturday	sábado
Hello	Hola
Good-bye	Adiós
Good morning	Buenos días
Good night	Buenas noches
Please	Por favor
Thank you	Gracias
How are you?	¿Cómo está?
Yes/No	Sí/No

INDEX

Acknowledgments
Book created for Highlights for Children, Inc., by Bender Richardson White.
Editor: Lionel Bender
Designer: Richard Johnson
Art Editor: Ben White
Picture Researcher: Cathy Stastny
Production: Kim Richardson

Map and flag produced by Stefan Chabluk.
Banknotes from Thomas Cook Currency Services.
Stamps from Stanley Gibbons.

Editorial Consultant: Andrew Gutelle
Ecuador Consultants: *Guide to Ecuador* was produced with the help of Fernando Luce, Ecuador Embassy, London; Roslyn Cameron; and Rosanna Rivadeneira Cordero.
Editorial Coordinator, Highlights for Children: Joan Hyman

Picture credits
SAP = South American Pictures Photo Agency, England; Corbis = Corbis Images, Inc.;
t = top, b = bottom, l = left, r = right.
Cover: Corbis/Hubert Stadler. Pages: 6-7, 7t: SAP/Tony Morrison. 7b: Corbis/Owen Franken. 8, 9t, 9b, 10-11, 11t, 11b: SAP/Tony Morrison. 12: Corbis/Michael and Patricia Fogden. 13t, 13b, 14l, 14-15: SAP/Tony Morrison. 15r: SAP/Kathy Jarvis. 16l: SAP/Tony Morrison. 16t: Corbis/Owen Franken. 17: Corbis/Pablo Corral. 18: SAP/Hilary Bradt. 19t: SAP/Peter Ryley. 19b: SAP/Sue Mann. 20, 21t, 21b: SAP/Tony Morrison. 22: SAP/Kimball Morrison. 23t: Corbis/Pablo Corral. 23b: SAP/Tony Morrison. 24-25: SAP/Edward Parker. 25t: Corbis/Jeremy Horner. 25b: SAP/Sarah Lazarus. 26: SAP/Kimball Morrison. 27t: SAP/Chris Sharp. 27b: Corbis/Wolfgang Kaehler. 28: SAP/Kathy Jarvis. 29, 30: SAP/Tony Morrison.
Illustration on page 1 by Tom Powers.